CATERPILLAR, COCOON, BUTTERFLY

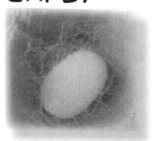

CATERPILLAR, COCOON, BUTTERFLY

OLIVIA M GRANT

authorHOUSE®

AuthorHouse™
1663 Liberty Drive
Bloomington, IN 47403
www.authorhouse.com
Phone: 1-800-839-8640

First published by AuthorHouse   11/21/2011

ISBN: 978-1-4678-8697-0 (sc)
ISBN: 978-1-4678-8591-1 (ebk)

Printed in the United States of America

Contents

CATERPILLAR
"THE END"

When something in our lives comes to "an end" we believe this sometimes to be a "tragic" period in our lives. We generally are not aware that the event can often be the pathway to reveal great new beginnings.

We never know what magic lies ahead. The caterpillar depicts how amazing transformation can be.

Divorce

A period of stress and trauma
High emotion spectacular drama

A time for tears to flow and flood
A time where you cannot be understood

A time to be lost and oh so lonely
A time to reflect upon "**if only**"

A time to call friends who don't want to know
A time to realise a whole new life to grow

A time to turn to god or your higher self-relief
Your trustworthy resource your personal belief

Always there for you good and bad
Always there for you happy and sad

Support is all you can take while you grieve
It is time that will heal, let your heart sorrow
leave

The Split

I have read books by the score
A hundred and more

All on self help
Positivity and believing

So why am I sad
Eternally grieving

Why can't I heal and move on with my life
Why do I struggle pain and strife

When will I turn my life around?

I am restless in pain
Feel I am going insane

The stress and the tension
Too painful to mention

The pain in my heart
Is heavy and dull

My cup is now empty
It used to be full

As the earth spins my insides churn
Happiness and laughter I longingly yearn

You split from the atom you shared your life
Your single now, no longer a wife

The tears spilled will soak the root
Life again will grow cute

Happiness will bloom and you will end the sorrow
It is just one corner you may turn it tomorrow

Truth

Live the truth
Do not live a lie
Keep your heart true
Do not let it die

If he lays down beside you
And you feel it is wrong
You have to start anew
And sing your happy song

You only have this one life
We do not know for how long
We should avoid trouble and strife
Be happy, be true, above all, belong

Hold Hands

Hold my hand, wipe my tears
Take me through the difficult years

Help me branch out and start over again
Ease my sorrow, ease my pain

I will survive, people do
And to myself I will remain true

You can't control another's behavior
You can ask for help from your trustworthy savior

Gossip

Please do not fan the flames of gossip my dear
Please do not believe all that you hear

No smoke without fire
You call me a liar

Gossip is distorted reality
Created by shallow tittle-tality

Think before joining the elaborate tale
Do not be a part of any hate mail

From one person to the next the story does grow
It cannot be all true -that we must know

So keep clear of the smoke, the flames and fire
Keep your respect the gossips will tire

With your head held high
Only the few know why

Jealousy

You can't have love without trust
It is essential—it is a must

Jealousy anger uncertainty
Means the end of you and me

So bad, so sad
In gone, move on

No good loving a jealous man
Destroy your life whenever he can

Excuses of love that wear you down
Time to get out of jealous town

I'm gone, moving on

Let go, let go, the answer is no
I will never return, I have to go

Life without you is free and good
Jealousy destroys all that it could

So enjoy love and trust
Clear the ashen dust

Live and love again
Sunshine laughter and rain

Return

Where have you been my lovely friend?
You seem to be lost and I want it to end

You are so talented, creative and true
Life has so much to offer you

You have to wake up with joy in your heart
Look at all the wonder you have played your part

Two amazing children—a girl and a boy
Now they are a source of incredible joy

Live for today and make opportunity
You absolutely have the total ability

Let the past end today and start over anew
Come back to this life and claim your good due

It may be invisible when clouds are grey
But joy is here—come back today

Husband

You were a good husband in your own way
Good and kind, loving every day

Your jealousy definitely wasn't any fun
A dangerous mind always pointing a gun

Hard working and dedicated to your son and
daughter
Often though not knowing and doing what you
didn't ought to

Thirty years passed by in a blink of an eye
Thought we would be together until the day we die

My blind faith in you was to be shook to the core
And we as a couple were truly no more

The Pearl wedding day was under a large black
cloud
And to celebrate this was not allowed

You didn't even acknowledge in any way
That's why I am convinced to part is okay

We must learn to exist in our new separate lives
Try to be kind stop throwing the knives

As tough as it has been I am growing well now
I am flourishing in all that I can allow

I will always have a special place for you in my
heart
Even though now we can only be happy apart

The children we have our are special gift
We must always work hard their spirits to lift

Despair

You wake in the morning and you just don't care
Your mind is full of sadness and despair

When did it come and get you—was it in your
dreams
Did it just appear, seeping through invisible
seams?

Despair so powerful to knock you off your feet
Stuck to your bed, crying under the sheet

How can it change so drastically from yesterday
How can it wipe your happiness away?

Despair is a force we have to fight
Win the battle it takes all your might

Throw back the sheet and paint on the smile
You will stronger in a short while

Keep the happy thoughts flowing fast and furious
Now your day will be just glorious

Crazy

People think I'm crazy
It is all so hazy

It happened in a heartbeat
Collapsed on my feet

All the years we had together
Thought it would be forever

Then suddenly a thunderbolt
Like a shot from a 22 colt

A flash of lightening
Shocking and frightening

So instant and quick
I was physically sick

What can you do
When they are untrue

It ended on the next heartbeat
Our life together in defeat

People think I'm crazy
It's all so hazy

Truth

Why do you stare at me alone
I am trying to be happy on my own

I don't think about you
Whether you are happy and true

Whether your partner is past the sell date
As you look at each other full of hate

I don't worry if you don't talk
With you I don't walk

I have no one to talk to but I am here to eat
My life is okay—truthful and complete

What could you say in retort?
Wish you had the strength to abort

This life of condemned misery
Daily washing over me

Se you see, I am not courageous like you
So to myself I must remain untrue

For One

For one yes please
They're ill at ease

Why can't we be alone?
Whets wrong with being on your own

For one—yes thanks just me, I sigh
How I was born and how I will die

If I am happy then can you not see
It is perfectly fine—let me be

Let me dine
Enjoy the red wine

Don't look and stare
Of course I care

It is much harder than it looks and it is our choice
As it is where we are with just our own voice

No one to talk to
No one to share
Doesn't mean feel free to stare!

Ownly

It happened its done
One life ended another begun

Part of a couple now on your own
Work on yourself not feeling alone

There's ownly and lonely
Two different things

Lonely is sad and destructive
Ownly is alone but constructive

Lonely you cant move a limb
Ownly you can do everything

On your own live life be a giver
Anything you want—Universe can deliver

So now lonely life of self-pity
Join the ownly committee

Live life to the full
Never be dull

Take the table
You are able

Lies

Lies I despise
Truth I adore

Hate is destruction
Love is construction

Jealousy is bad energy
Trust is true synergy

Joy is the way
To enjoy every day

Begin

It does not matter the reason why
You are on your own it is okay to cry

Begin the begin—starting again
Take a step a day—accept the pain

Every day grief and sorrow
You can find another tomorrow

You can't waste your life away
You have to face another day

It is a grief stricken time
No sense, no reason, no rhyme

Begin the begin—start again
Live again, sunshine and rain

Sunshine is warmth for the core
Rain is precious water, a resource to draw

Sunshine and rain—a rainbow
Happiness will from within re-grow

Be strong have trust and faith
Come back and join the human race
With a stronger happier face

Aura

Get out of my aura, get out of my space
Your history now, get out of my face

Get out of my dreams
Get out of my hair
Your history now—I do not care

Get out of my bank account
Get out of my house
You were my lover now you're a louse

You crawl on with your life
I am no longer your wife

I do not need a bug, no warmth in a hug

I need a trustworthy partner with a beautiful aura
Who truly lays down his life and says I adore her!

COCOON
"MIDDLE"

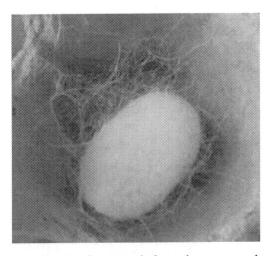

The period of your life when you know there is no turning back and you have to refocus your mind to the path ahead.

Moving out of the shelter of your sad and cosy cocoon. Ready to emerge and dust yourself down

Cocoon

In the Cocoon
Wrapped in spun silk
Time to attune
Leave the spilt milk

The wounds can heal
Safe and warm
Life to reveal
A whole new dawn

Grow stronger
Warm cosy nest
Try not to stay longer
Just enjoy the rest

Emerge revitalised
Head held high
Feeling energised
Want to live not die

The cocoon has spun
To save the day
I have won
Back to play

Moving On

Its time to move on
Go forward and grow
Its time to belong
Its time you know

It will be good for you
Just trust in god, have belief
And this will be true
The end of all your grief

I cannot wait for the Diva to return
She's the best you know
From life she did adjourn
But now its time to show

The true and talented person she is
So kind and wonderful
Life and soul—true bucks fizz
Make life bountiful

The world is your oyster be a Diva
The time is now 2010
So lets celebrate the new with eager
Find your perfect den

Lots of love to my special friend

Connect

A new era in humankind
Leave the past behind
Start afresh begin anew
Claim the life you are due

Turn off the TV abandon Jeremy Kyle
It is sick, sad and rather vile
Leave Lorraine Kelly
More to life than Telly

Go walking and connect with the ground
Notice all that grows around
Hug a tree—gain some strength
Gain energy for that extra length

Eat fresh, well and enjoy yourself
You will be a picture of health

Listen, read, learn and grow
You will know the seeds to sow

Utopia

You get what you wish for
Yes it is true

Every thought contributes
For me and you

Control your thoughts
To all that you desire

Life will be great
Vibration level higher

Into the vortex you should go
Nurture the seeds you did sow

In no time at all the seeds will flourish
You will water maintain and nourish

UTOPIA is the place your heading "the dream'
When you arrive you will surely feel "reem"

My Heart

My new shock status in life
Means I am no longer a wife

I want my heart to sing out loud
Feel alive and proud

If love makes the world go round
Then love will have to be found

I have to remove the fear
Get myself into gear

Rejoin life and have me some fun
2011 the year I begun

Yes I am loving, gifted and kind
And still a treasure for someone to find

Clean

Bursts open the windows and start to clean
The shiniest home you have ever seen

Birds are singing the day is good
Perfect for a walk in the wood

Nature is calling but chores to do
The sound of dogs barking and cock-a-doodle-do

Cup of green tea and no more excuses and cackle
Work has to be done get on and tackle

Then the reward is mine to take
A simple walk around the lake

A little treat too for being such a goody
A cappuccino at the lakeside cafe with your buddy

Jump For Joy

The leap of your life
Jump long. Jump high

Jump for joy
Do not be coy

Jump for fun
Then run and run

Jump even higher on the trampoline
Jump so high you cannot be seen

When you land we will know
That was the jump that helped you grow!

Love To Live

I love to work I love to play
I love to have energy every day

I love to eat fresh and organic
I live a life that is pretty manic

I love my family who have flown the nest
I love my granddaughter she is the best

I love nature so proud and so strong
By the lake strolling is where I belong

I love the sea and oceans blue
Takes me on adventures finding places anew

We need to breathe fully and enjoy our lives
Before the end when death arrives

Too late them to do all you love and desire
Live today, live now do not smoulder, be on fire!

Positive Thought

Everything happening in your life starts with a
thought
So the positive plus sign is the one to court

Keep the negative in minus—send it away
Don't give it any airtime in any one-day

Negative = minus — will dreams take away
Positive = plus + will bring gifts to stay

The power is in the mind
To all treasure you wish to find

Awake

When you wake early
Get up and at it

If you can't sleep
You have to admit

Days are short
Time is precious

Don't waste an hour
Life is delicious

A busy body is alive
A busy body will grow and thrive

If you wake in the black of the night
Do not lie there in fright

Jump out of bed read a book
Or play one on audio, listen not look

Never focus on lack of sleep
Do not bother to count the sheep

Every single waking hour
Enjoy life enjoy the power

Angel Dream Stream

So I am in this beautiful bubble of life
Where I no longer have to strife

Bubble where no room for pathetic
The bubble where my mind is poetic

Where I can only be kind
To all the people I come to find

Where I have the strength
To go to any length

Where I can create all I need
Ability for anything—yes indeed

My heart is beating oh so fast
As I have now left my past

The future is spiraling frighteningly ahead
The future by my super-team, I am being led

My team is Angel Dream Stream
Who all my desires through them beam

My team and I burst with pride
As we sell our book, far and wide

Sunlight

Light up my life
Light up my world

The sunlight is here
Yes its unfurled

It is warm and bright
We are all alight

The green is greener
The land looks cleaner

My eyes see clearer
Joy is much nearer

Keep me warm keep me glowing
Keep me nurtured keep me growing

The more I relax with the flow
The better my life does go

The more I bathe in sunshine
The more life is truly divine

Win Or Lose

You can be a winner or loser—you choose
Choose anything you want—talent will ooze

Apply don't deny is the only cry
The resource is abundant just wet the dry

Seize the day—seize your life
Claim it back from the struggle and strife

Have fun, live love and laughter
Stop being so serious be a little dafter

Exploration, adventure, taste and desire
Of all things new, never ever tire

Life is a journey of universal design
All on this planet is yours and mine

Love Is Free

Life is good so many pleasures
Life is good so full of treasures

It is true the best things in life are free
Simply walking in the fresh air for me

Life is what you make it—good old saying
Be happy be grateful always praying

Have integrity be kind and giving
Get the best of life through honest living

A picnic in the park by the lake
A simple pleasure free to take

Running, walking, laughing and singing
All make your heart uplifted and zinging

Love is the best feeling of all
Enjoy your life—stand up tall

Banish Hate

I need a lover I need a mate
I want to banish all of the hate

I want to light up my lover's eyes
Share life the joy and the ties

Come to me now
I am waiting and ready
It takes time, the how to be steady

By my angel my special date
From the Universe my soul mate

Baby Angel Feather

The teeniest tiniest white feather you could ever
see
Landed third finger left hand on me

This is a message special and true
How do I receive it, what do I do

Open your heart, listen from inside
Keep ears and eyes open wide

The message will be strong and clear
For only you have been chosen to hear

The elite baby angel message is on its way
Prepare yourself for a very special day

A clear thought you have previously conveyed
Is going to be honored, it is being portrayed

It will land on you like a surprise
You are chosen—you are happy and wise

BUTTERFLY "BEGIN"

It is time to emerge from the cocoon and start life anew – spread our fragile new butterfly wings

Reward

Life is rewarding if you care
The planet is giving
We must share

Energy flows freely
For each and all
We just have to see
To keep the trees tall

The planet abundance is the sign
Providing resource—truly divine

Here is your seed
Nurture it well
And the planet indeed
Will grow all that you dwell

Air

I look out of my window today
The fog has gone away

The day is bright and still
The fresh air my daily pill

Walking and yoga my agility
Empowering my brain, thought and ability

Oh beautiful bright day
What have you got coming my way

Nothing but good you can fly
Join the birds I hear you cry

I feel the vigor and joy too
My time for success is definitely due

You have success take a look around
Beauty and treasure do you surround

Be happy and grateful your cup overflows
Your strength and beauty burns and glows

True Love

True love you will find
True love the best kind

Loving and giving
Dedicated and true

Happy and living
For him and for you

You will make each other happy
That I am sure

Free independent spirits
Whom each other adore

Love and trust is the recipe
You need
Pure happiness ensues
Yes indeed

In each other company, sheer delight
Together to set the world alight!

Burning Desire

Burning desire
Take you higher

Faith and belief
To achieve

Imagination to win
Integrity no sin

Attain knowledge
Appropriate college

Always plan
Then you can

Don't waste the ride
Be sure to decide

Those who persist
The universe cannot resist!

Can't Stop Me Now

You can't stop me now
I'm on a rock and roll
You can't stop me now
I'm achieving my goal

I am writing with a fashion
A natural flowing passion
I'm on my way you know
Where I aimed to go

A bestseller no less is all I ask
I am here to do the task

I will keep going
My book will be growing

My journey will end
I will make the last bend

Over the line
My book is divine!

Have It All

You can have it all
You can balance the ball

One two three or four
Even some more

As long as they are in the air
You are on the path to somewhere

Drop one and still continue on
You will still get to where you belong

You can have it all
Just balance the ball!

Opportunity

Opportunity may knock at your door
You didn't hear it, the time before

Opportunity has to be sought
And it cannot be bought

Opportunity is always possible
Opportunity knocks yet it is inaudible

How do we get some of the "O"
Plenty of seeds you have to sew

Set the ground ahead
Abundant flowerbed

Then when its time you know
The opportunity will sh'O'w

Olivia M Grant

Money Tree

My money doesn't grow on a tree
It flows to me from the Sea

The Pacific Ocean to be precise
Flowing strong it is very nice

Plenty for everyone and some more
Fulfill our dreams by the score

Over and over it will never stop
All that you want, shop till you drop

Achieve your dreams don't let them expire
The universe provides all you can desire

Quantum Leap

I want to take a Quantum Leap
Out of the shallow into the deep

Take some risk and take a chance
It is my time to dance

Time to arrive where I wish to be
To claim all that due and meant for me

Angels

Angels fly
In the sky

Here to guide
By our side

Here to sense
Be intense

Lose inhibition
Follow intuition

Belief is all it takes
To have our angel cakes

They are always here
To protect and love us dear

Love your angels in the sky
And you may find that you can fly!

Quality Street

Is health more important that wealth?
I think so

Is money more important than milk and honey
Maybe so

I happiness more important than snappiness
Absolutely so

In energy more important than synergy
I am sure so

Is personality more important than reality
Could be so

Is kindness more important than selfishness?
Definitely so

Is caring more important than sharing
Could be the same though

Is giving the key to good living
Absolutely, definitely, I am convinced so!

Joy

I want abundant joy
I know it is not a toy
It is a special feeling
Happy and healing

It is the place to be
For you and for me
Health and joy your goal
Sign up now, enroll

Health, wealth and bliss
The reward for seeing this

Visionary, joyous, nurtured and inspired
You are well and truly hired

Passionate, enthusiastic with total belief
You can all join us, what a relief!

Ocean

Two thirds of planet earth
Is soaking in our wonderful ocean

One third of the planet earth is land and motion

I love the land
I love the water

I love life
We really ought to

We can swim and sail the ocean
We can walk, enjoy the earth

We can fly the world in motion
And constantly rebirth

Enjoy, live life, love laugh
Never ever have enough

Always strive to arrive
Keep your joy in you alive

FINAL SELECTION

COSMIC "BUTTERFLY FREEDOM OF THE UNIVERSE"

God
Of The Majestic
Mountains

God of the majestic mountains—Tell me your story
As you stand tall and proud in all your glory

Storing your treasures of diamonds and gold
No wonder you are so strong and bold

You are mineral rich with crowns of snow
And down you precious waters flow

You have minerals too, copper and iron
A place for Juanita to be buried and die on

Granite marble and stone
Rubies too you enthrone

Boulders, formations and shapes
Down the colourful mountain snapes

Majestic Mountains what else to unfold
What other buried treasures do you behold

Something powerful and special I am sure
Oh mighty majestic mountains with treasures
galore!

Treasure Trove

Crystal is a gorgeous and amazing jewel
Rubies are so red—just like fire fuel

Diamonds are so shiny and strong
To be without would be wrong

Golden nuggets shine so bold
Molten silver ours to mould

Sapphire blue reflects the ocean
Opal too a delicate potion

Emeralds bold and green
All to own someone's dream

Gems and stones from our Earth's treasure
Giving us endless grateful pleasure

Nuclear

We have seen the second evidence of a nuclear
disaster
Mother Nature will never ever have a master

She doesn't like what man is doing
So our lives she will ruin

Clean up our act and treasure our planet
Before she decides no one is capable to man it

She is woman and we know she will win
Man must stop all this sin

She wants integrity, respect, kindness and giving
Then Mother Nature will let us all go on living!

Missiles Again!

Oh my god . . . not more missiles again
Showering Libya rockets of rain

What can a missile achieve?
Murder, sadness and humans to grieve

Death destruction the world gone mad
We deal with the fallout equally bad

What happened to peace and caring for all
Why can't we love and be kind big or small

The planet must unite
To earn Mother Nature's respite

She is HELL BENT
We must all RELENT

Solar System

Mercury Saturn, Pluto and Mars
All surrounded by billions of stars

Saturn, Uranus, Neptune and Venus
No one out there has ever seen us

Here on planet earth
We are the only ones to give birth

We live in abundance divine
Thanks to the wonderful sunshine

We have the moon to light our night
Beautiful beams to keep our sight

Of thank you Universe—it's quite a projection
The solar system—total collection

Milky Way

As I look to the galaxy to spot the Milky Way
All I see is the moon full and bright, lighting my way

I cannot see any stars tonight I know they are there
I wanted to see the constellation, the great bear

I saw the planet Venus as clear as night
Together with the moon shining very bright

I saw a star arrangement too
From the glorious mountain top in Peru
It was a wonderful blanket of stars
The moon, Jupiter and Mars

Solar system vast and diverse
Earth thanking you wonderful universe!

Explore

I want to find something new
Never seen before
I want to find a key
To a never opened door
I want to explore!

I want to find something
For all to adore
Spectacular and breathtaking
I want to explore!

I want it to be magnificent
I want an encore
Please keep it coming
I want more to ensure

EXPLORE

Sail

I went on a holiday to learn how to sail
My first day at sea in an eight-force gale

My life in the skippers hand as we heavily keeled
No seasickness though happily revealed

My good friend Jo a great crew friend
Definitely thought our lives would end

Sailing improved, we got into our stride
Good sailors were we enjoying the ride

Leeward ho, the skipper orders away the sail
Tacking starboard, as the winds prevail

Anchors away—we end another day
Moored to enjoy a glass of wine in the bay

Dinner tonight as we step onto land
We jolly sailors make a great band

Tomorrow well be off at knots
On our beautiful sailing yachts

Pacha mamma

Mother nature can strike you dead
With a lighting bolt through your head

She can kill one or thousands, its her choice
Earthquake and Tsunami in her loud voice

250,000 people killed in an hour
Oh she is mighty and oh she has power

She can be kind and giving too
Providing all the food for me and you

She is responsible for everyone living
We need her to be forgiving

We must do what she desires
If we don't want our forest fires

We must care for the planet good
If we don't want to ensure constant flood

We want good food, flowers and trees
All creatures great, the birds and the bees

We want the rainbow with the pot of gold
Then lets be good and do what we're told!

Force Of Nature

Gravity space
Human race

Mother nature very old
Force of nature still so bold

13.7 billion years she celebrates
How diverse—still no entrance gates

Galaxies, stars, billions out there
All we do is stand and stare

There is no force in the universe
More powerful than nature

Respect

Zero G

We take a flight to zero G
Throttle back explore no gravity

We float around with no control
Not a joyride—rock and roll

Gravity just gone away
Cancelled out today

A speck of dust, a great big star
I like my feet on the ground by far

Ocean Bed

I stood on the bed of the ocean
40m below sea level—no motion

The bed of the planet earth
Some weights around my girth

I am so close to the core
I am in total awe

I have an oxygen tank
My breath is in a bank

Without it I would die
It is worth the risk I cry

Special and privileged is how I feel
To swim the ocean with turtle and eel

Where corals are formed and grow
And all the sea creatures puff and glow

Sea horses and clown fish galore
Diving the ocean I absolutely adore!

Ocean Spa-Cific

In going to the ocean again
Pure sunshine holiday no rain

The island of Hawaii—a jewel in the Pacific
My order there is very spa-cific

Health happiness and a time divine
Beautiful food and plentiful wine

It is my ocean of abundance galore
I will be filling my mack-truck with more and more

Overflowing and growing I will return
With all my wealth, I did rightfully earn

Crystal energy

On planet earth send me crystal energy—core to
core
Through the Universe I want to soar

Divine energy—a treasured gift
Soar me over the African rift

Take me to the Barrier Reef
Over the ocean—over the heath

Soaring high, like a bird of prey
Anywhere I want—I am on my way

Onwards and onwards is where I am heading
Universe and I—a crystal wedding

The power is ours to use as we wish
Travel health and happiness is my ordered dish

Tsunami

Oh my god—disaster in Japan
Mother nature or dangerous man

Tsunami and quakes
The land floods and shakes

A nuclear disaster about to blow
Who the hell the man this seed did sow

Man woman and child wiped away
Will not live to see another day

Why what did they do why did they die
Nothing I know of, its manmade I cry

When will they stop their greed I ask?
Lets make them now lets put to task

Green and caring is our way to go
Please lets continue our planet to grow

Give

Live is for living
Be kind and giving

Never be hateful
Always be grateful

Enjoy each day
Come what may

The law of attraction
Is all about action

The more you have to give
The more you are productive

The more you believe
The more you receive

Give all you have all of the time
And so your life shall be divine

Karma

At the moment the nation may feel crime does pay
The criminals are rich and powerful
They do not care it is their job night and day

What the criminal does not know
Is that he cannot be happy
He has no seeds to sow

What the victims cannot see and understand
Is justice being served?
Where is their helping hand?

Good over evil should be the key
We must make the effort for all to see

More good than bad
Has to rule
Stop this crime
And ridicule

Take every penny from the criminals' coffers
Put it to use to fight crime
And lets get many more coppers

Whatever it takes, Lets put the work in
Unite the good people, we will win

Sunshine

The sun is shining today
Feel better in every way

The sky is so vivid blue
Green grass covered in dew

Flowers a colourful blaze
Upon which I am drawn to gaze

Yes go on get out there
Quick wash and brush my hair

Trainers on ready to go
Join this free spectacular show

Best things in life are truly free
Available to everyone—you and me

Imagination

A rainbow of pearls and rubies too
Gold, silver, satin and sapphires blue
v
Emerald green providing a sheen
Diamond sparkle set the scene

Grass the colour of sand a golden glow
Emerald tree trunks and leaves in a bow

Turtle-doves in opal shimmer
A sapphire dolphin with a swimmer

Copper benches by the Coral Sea
Flowerbeds in the shape of a key

Lets paint the picture take a look
Don't forget the golden duck

The horizon can be all you in your vision
Your imagination is freedom from prison

Your mind is not under lock and key
Release it, imagine, let it run free

Of course we can have a purple tree!

Peru

You must visit Peru
For a minimum of a week or two

Arrive in Lima City
The fountains are so pretty

Visit my abundant Pacific Ocean
The sights are a magical potion

Drive on to Pisco—Pelicans and Penguins
To the desert oasis—sandboard down the
mountains

Colca Canyon see the Condor
Five metre span above you they soar

Floating islands on Lake Titicaka
Superfood, purple corn and Maca

Traditional clothes and simple lifestyle
Everyone happy with a wonderful smile

The best is the City of Cusco
Somewhere I feel you must go

High in the Andean mountains
In the square with the magnificent fountains

Look up to the sky
Statue Jesus watching you up high

Destination Inca trail
More adventure to unveil

14,000 feet closer to the sky
In your tent nice and dry

Maccu-Piccu is the aim
Arriving there is all to gain

Magnificent spectacular—blown away
The inca's were incredible I have to say

Olivia M Grant

Still more to come and onto the plane we bungle
Were heading off to the Amazon jungle

Catch a boat down the River
In the Amazon—I start to quiver

Monkeys in the trees howling loud as we float
Snakes, otters and Cayman swim close to the boat

The tropical heat, the sounds of the jungle
Makes you feel glad and oh so humble

Peru is one astounding adventure
The most amazing memories forever to picture

Take advantage of this jewel of South America
Go and give thanks and bless the INCA

Hawaii

Hawaii is my dream destination
The pearl of the US nation

A string of jewels 2000 miles from distant land
Mainly Polynesian culture to hand

Maui, Ohau, Big Island too
Volcanoes erupting molten spew

Tropical Rainforest, black ash beach
Gigantic waterfalls out of reach

The hula hula is a magical sight
Dancing grass skirts in a dusky light

Gigantic waves frothing and crashing
Waikiki surfers taking a little bashing

Sunrise and sunsets to completely adore
Pineapples, sugar and Coffee growing galore

Every bend, every turn - a wonderful sight
Hawaii sets my life alight